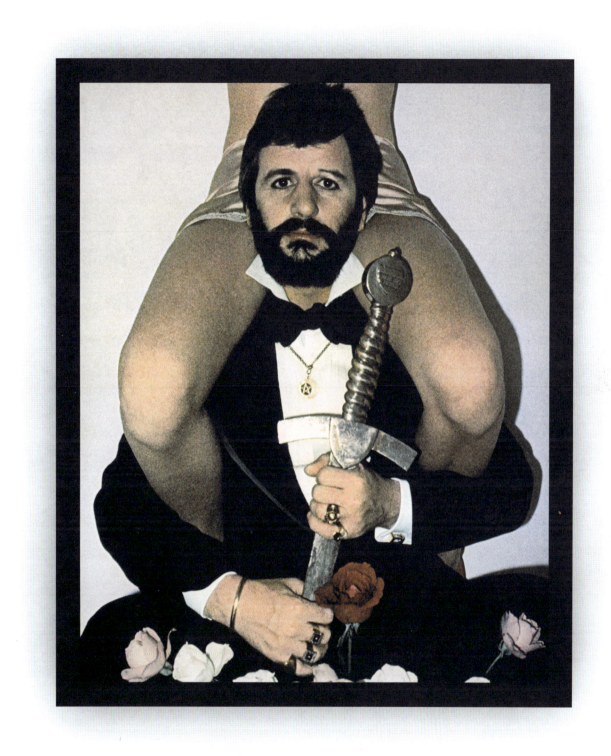

For Annette —
  Enjoy the 70s — again —
through my eyes — a girl with a camera —
and used it!! Keep Rockin!!

            Much love & happiness,

                  Nancy
                   ♡
                  xx

        Nancy Lee Andrews

A Dose of Rock 'n' Roll

Nancy Lee Andrews

A Dose of Rock 'n' Roll

by Nancy Lee Andrews

Published 2008

ISBN: 978-1-85443-230-8

Printed and bound in
Singapore by Star Standard

for the publisher

Dalton Watson Fine Books
1730 Christopher Drive,
Deerfield, IL 60015,
USA

www.daltonwatson.com

Contents

Acknowledgments

To all who appear in this book – without you there would be no book. Thank you for being a part of my life no matter how small or large. You brought me joy when I took your picture and I hope it brings forth a smile if you see yourself on these pages.

Richard Starkey, with whom I shared the 1970s. You showed me the world through your eyes and I learned to understand it with my own. Without you it would not have been as exciting. Thank you for the memories: it was the roller coaster ride of my life.

Lee, Jason and Zak, you brightened my life and gave me unconditional love. Our time together has a place in my heart. You are the closest I have come to having children of my own.

Marshall Terrill, my editor, for guiding me through the maze and pulling it all together when I was all over the map. Your experience is golden and your friendship means the world to me. Thank you for your fathomless knowledge of every facet of rock 'n' roll.

Glyn Morris, my publisher, who was there by my side through thick and thin and catching every little mistake before we went to press. Thank you for putting up with me while we hashed it out at all hours of the day and night. I couldn't have a better publisher. What would we do without Skype?

Ben Gibbs, what a computer warrior you are when it comes to art direction. The fact that you were available to talk to me at ten o'clock at night (London time) still brings a smile to my face. Thank you.

Pattie Boyd, for breaking the mold and paving the way for the ladies. Your pictures are treasures.

May Pang, for your picture of John and your long lasting friendship.

Mario Casciano, you clever man, thank you for the title, *A Dose of Rock 'n' Roll.*

To Emmy Harris for your loving friendship and taking me to garage sales when I thought I would lose my mind if I had to sit in front of the computer one more minute.

To Lynn and Rusty Russell, true friends who believed I could do this and who fed my husband and me on those nights when I was too tired to cook. Lynn, you make the best Caesar salad!

To Cathy and Doug Soref, who believed and encouraged me to go for my dreams. Your love and generosity have made me a better person.

Andee Nathanson, my soul sister, who has been there for me since the beginning of time. Your words of wisdom and humor keep me centered. We have been through the '70s, '80s, '90s, and now it's 2008. And we still have the teens, '20s, '30s and '40s ahead of us.

Eddie Barnes, my husband, my rock and my sanctuary. You are my better half and I love you. Without your perceptive understanding and endless support I could not have completed this project. I can't imagine life without you.

Nancy Lee Andrews – 2008

Introduction

Music has been a part of my life for as long as I can remember. My mother always had the radio on or was spinning records on our old Victrola. Hank Snow, Ray Charles, Connie Francis, Frank Sinatra, Fats Domino, Glenn Miller, The Platters, Doris Day, Johnny Horton, Marty Robbins, Hank Williams, Elvis. You can see where I'm going with this…I was raised on the music of the '40s and '50s, from big bands to country to blues to crooners. Then my era kicked in – the watershed '60s and the funky '70s.

The British Invasion, mixed with the homegrown sounds of good ol' American rock, gave me an ocean of music to swim in and explore. It was the undercurrent, the driving force behind everything I did. In the summer of 1967, I ventured to Manhattan to see if I could make some money modeling and was picked up right away by the Eileen Ford Agency. I started working and living in the city, going to plays, musicals and dance clubs.

When the Fillmore East, the old Village Theatre, opened in March of 1968 it changed my world. That's where I met and socialized on the weekends with the young melodic geniuses like The Doors, Jimi Hendrix, Jefferson Airplane, Mountain, The Grateful Dead, Taj Mahal and so on. As I arrived with my model friends in our go-go boots, mini-dresses, false eye lashes, pale pink lipstick and long hair falls (just like the fashion today), Michael Klenfner was more than happy to open the back door. Michael went on to become the grand poobah of marketing in the music business and an executive with Atlantic Records.

The 1970s was a time of great discovery and creativity. I worked with the preeminent photographers of the day – Avedon, Milton Greene, Bert Stern, Irving Penn and James Houghton – spending weeks posing for catalogs or filming television commercials. Increasingly however, over the years, I became more interested in the other side. The process was fascinating, from the click of the shutter to holding a print in my hand.

I was helping Milton Greene rinse prints in the darkroom one day, asking too many questions, as usual, when he said it was time for me to start shooting. He gave me a Nikon camera and some film and told me to capture anything that I found interesting. I loved it! I remember him looking over my first contact sheet and smiling, giving me praise and telling me, "You've got an eye, Nancy." His guidance and words encouraged me to continue.

My first love, musician Carl Radle, was the eminent bass player with Leon Russell, Eric Clapton and George Harrison to name a few luminaries on his resume, was passionate about photography. He was technically proficient with the camera and shared his knowledge with me. Our idea of a vacation was going to the desert and photographing nature. Occasionally I would accompany him on tour and take pictures for my own amusement of the band while in concert or behind the scenes.

My second love, Ringo Starr, was also ardent about photography which was a huge part of our life as evidenced in the pages of this book. Ringo was a constant source of support. He encouraged me to become a better photographer and gave me plenty of professional opportunities. We collaborated on two of his album covers, *Ringo the 4th* and *Bad Boy* as well as the advertising shoot for "Ringo", a TV special that aired in 1978.

A camera was never far from my grasp. Many a night was spent making dinner and setting up the slide projector to entertain our friends with the latest batch of images from our journeys to foreign lands. Capturing images of family, friends and travel was my passion, and is reflected in *Λ Dose of Rock 'n' Roll.*

Turning these pages you will travel on a journey through the most thrilling time of my life. It spans approximately ten years but it was a decade that marked extraordinary times and the vanguard of our musical icons of today. The images in this book are personal and intimate and include some of our greatest musicians; some thriving today, some are sadly no longer with us. Looking into the faces of Keith Moon and Harry Nilsson, and remembering their animated personalities and astonishing talent which is now being discovered by a new generation of music lovers, gives me tremendous joy.

Compiling this book has been very cathartic for me. It's like looking through a family photo album with memories flooding my mind as if it were only yesterday that I clicked the shutter…seeing how young the children were and knowing that now they are parents and their parents who grace these pages are grandparents and so on. Life…it is a brilliant cycle.

Carl capturing the sunrise in Joshua
Tree National Monument, California.

Carl Radle

Carl Radle was more than just my first love: he was a friend, a teacher, fellow artist and a guiding light who took me by the hand and led me through the insane world of rock 'n' roll.

Carl is one of those musical figures who has almost been forgotten save for a few hip journalists and hardcore followers of rock. He was an influential bassist, a musician's musician and the original "Ace of Bass." Carl played on a number of gold and platinum singles and albums by Eric Clapton, George Harrison, Joe Cocker, Art Garfunkel, Rita Coolidge, Leon Russell, Dave Mason, J.J. Cale and Muddy Waters. Carl also toured and recorded with some of the greatest acts of the 1960s and 1970s, including Gary Lewis and the Playboys, Delaney & Bonnie, Derek and the Dominos and the epic Joe Cocker, *Mad Dogs and Englishmen* tour, which was the largest concert of its time.

Rock stars dating models today is a cliché, but in the early '70s it was a new pairing. I fell into it when the Fillmore East opened for business in March 1968. The old concert hall, located in the East Village, was a world unto itself. I'd step through that door and it was like the other side of Alice's looking glass. It hosted both prominent and up-and-coming bands of the time, from The Doors, The Byrds, The Who, Jefferson Airplane and Janis Joplin to blues and avant-garde acts as well.

On this particular night Leon Russell was on the bill with a young piano player, Elton John, as his opening act. I was in the hallway just outside a dressing room when someone bumped into me. It was Leon Russell's bass player, Carl Radle. As soon as Carl looked at me I knew my modeling days were numbered. He was unlike anyone I had ever met. He was a kind, sweet soul, who was funny, smart and a guru to all close to him. He had a wisdom that belied his years and was generous in imparting it whenever asked. His low-key personality mirrored how he played his instrument – minimally but a driving force, the backbone of the band.

We led an exciting life, touring and recording almost non-stop with the biggest names in the music industry. When we weren't on the road, we settled into a quiet life in Tulsa, Oklahoma, where Carl was born. His love of photography was something that we shared. Having been on the other side of the camera for years, I now made a serious leap with his help. We spent days driving across country and capturing nature with our dueling cameras. He had a gentle eye for color, composition and natural light.

My family was torn away from me at a young age and Carl was the first man with whom I wanted to create what I sorely missed. My path was always to give way to love and Carl made me feel safe and protected. In return, I nurtured him. We were building a future together until his addictive nature took over. It was eventually too powerful for us to overcome.

His death in 1980 at the age of thirty-seven was a surprise. He had died of a kidney infection caused by the use of alcohol and narcotics. Even though we hadn't been together for years I felt as though someone ripped my heart out and threw it into the deepest part of the ocean. They say time heals all wounds… not completely…they are still tender.

Left: Eric Clapton at Stonehenge, 1970.
Photo: Carl Radle.

Above: Chuck Blackwell, drummer, and Carl following Leon Russell's direction. California, July 1971.

Left: Tequila quenches the thirst on a hot California day.

Above right: Carl always
had a bass in his hands.

Right: Joshua Tree National
Monument, California.

Above: Carl on a sunny day at an open air concert in Anaheim, California July 1971.

Above right: The band had just arrived in Hawaii for a Leon Russell concert and immediately plopped onto the beach.

Right: An adventure in the Californian desert. I loved my Nikon camera and those purple suede boots.

Bill Graham

Bill Graham was all the things you've probably read or heard about: fiery, loud, cantankerous, difficult and competitive. He was also a wonderful man.

The promoter was a father figure to many rock acts but he reminded me more of a foreman in charge of the docks. I remember him cursing vehemently at one of the roadies and turning around and saying to me sweetly, "Are you okay, honey? Do you have everything you need?" This Jekyll and Hyde display of character took me aback, but that moment summed up Bill Graham in a nutshell.

Looking back decades later and finally knowing Bill's history, it's easy to forgive his actions. Born Wolfgang Granjonza in 1931, he escaped Nazi Germany to grow up in a Bronx, New York foster home. At eighteen, he anglicized his name to Bill Graham when he spotted it in the phonebook. A few years later he headed west to San Francisco, where he promoted legendary shows at the Fillmore West for Jefferson Airplane, The Grateful Dead, Frank Zappa, Santana, Janis Joplin, Hot Tuna and Country Joe and the Fish. I saw a lot of those late '60s shows at the Fillmore because I was dating Chick Casady, whose brother, Jack was the bass player in Jefferson Airplane. My backstage access enabled me to watch Bill in action many nights.

Tough but fair would be the best way to characterize Bill. If he was challenged, he would look it up in the contract, and if he found he had made a mistake, he was quick to admit it and correct the situation.

Artists loved Bill because he did things right. He genuinely cared about their music and production values and was not a quick-buck promoter. Bill's particular gift was bringing the performer and audience together, I guess it made him the midwife of the modern-day rock concert.

Even though I was supposed to be a fly on the wall at a 1972 Leon Russell concert in Palo Alto, California, Bill knew I was taking his picture. To his credit, Bill didn't change his personality or go into freeze mode like most subjects who aren't used to the camera. It was business as usual and he was barking orders in no time. Treating people too gently was not one of his personality traits. The best description of Bill I can think of is that he was a beloved dictator.

1931~1991

Leon Russell

At the height of his career, Leon Russell was the Elmer Gantry of rock 'n' roll.

I don't know what Leon's religious affiliation was, but it's apparent the Oklahoma native had been raised in the church – the fire and brimstone type. On stage, he revved crowds into a frenzy, emulating an evangelist on the pulpit. He was mesmerizing, creating a swaying atmosphere that delivered the audience into the palm of his hand...me included. The interesting dichotomy about Leon is that he's completely different off stage.

I can say that, because I've known Leon for years but I never got close to him. I've cooked for him, fed him, been with him in the studio for days at a time and was part of his tour entourage in the early '70s. His bass player, Carl Radle, was my boyfriend. Leon never gave me anything more than a perfunctory smile and "Miss Nancy". It was as if we were in a silent movie together – players in a diverse cast but there was no dialogue with each other. The reason for that could have been my relationship with Carl, who possibly told Leon I was off limits. I happen to think it's due to the fact that Leon is one of those individuals who gives everything on stage and may have nothing left afterwards. He's like a Jack O' Lantern – when you blow out the candles, there's only shadow and smoke.

I'll give Leon this: he's a brilliant artist and has written some of the greatest songs of our time. I happened to be in the recording studio when he penned "Tight Rope" from the *Carney* album. A moment of inspiration took over him at the control booth and he wrote the lyrics on a brown paper bag. Three hours later, the song was in the can and turned out to be one of the biggest hits of his career.

Fast forward almost fifteen years later. The two of us hadn't seen each other since the early '70s. I was boarding a plane from New York to Moscow. Leon and several other artists were headlining a concert to help raise money for The Children's Trust. The proceeds were going to be donated to several orphanages in Russia. I was the official photographer documenting the event for all the publicity. As I walked down the aisle of the plane, I spotted Leon in his seat and stroking his beard, deep in thought behind his sunglasses. I was excited to see him so I stopped and said hello. He looked up long enough to acknowledge me. "Hi, Miss Nancy," he said blankly. And that was it! After an awkward moment of silence, I continued to my seat.

We were in Russia for ten days, and Leon didn't say boo to me. That was amazing given the fact that I took publicity shots of him, Edgar Winter and LaToya Jackson in the middle of Red Square. I shouldn't have felt bad, though. He didn't converse with Edgar or LaToya either.

In the strangest twist of all, Leon moved to Nashville about a decade ago and we are practically neighbors. Neither one of us has extended a dinner invitation.

Left: Leon loved to wear exaggerated top hats like this one in 1971.

Above: Leon backstage after a performance. 1971.

Left: Edgar Winter and LaToya Jackson with Leon for a publicity shot in Red Square, Moscow 1987.

Right: Leon in Red Square in front of Ivan the Terrible's tribute to himself.

Left: Leon performing in concert, Moscow, 1987.

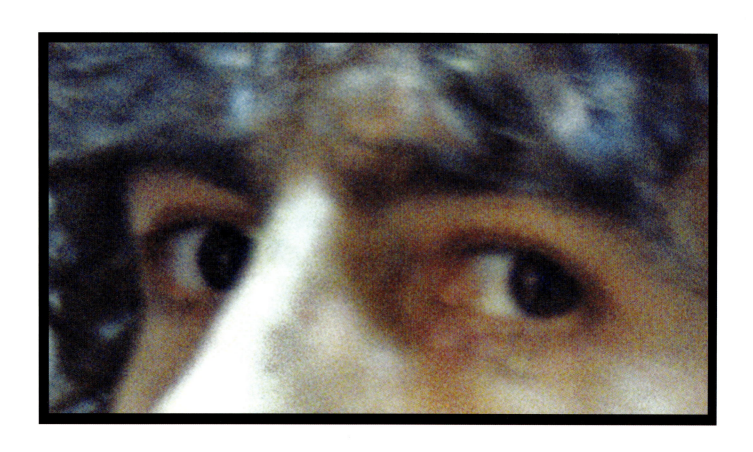

George Harrison

They say that still waters run deep. It took time to receive an invitation from George Harrison to allow you into the end of the pool that was mostly reserved for his music.

I first met George backstage at *The Concert for Bangla Desh* in August 1971. I was dating Carl Radle, who had appeared on George's *All Things Must Pass* and had just finished recording with Derek and the Dominos.

My connection with George happened gradually. I bonded with his first wife, the lovely Pattie Boyd and came to know George better when he signed a deal in mid-1973 with A&M Records, which distributed his Dark Horse record label. That was the big buzz at the company – "We've got a Beatle on the lot." At the time I was working for Lou Adler at Ode Records, which was part of A&M. We used to call the lot a "music school campus." As well as setting up offices, George was getting ready for his 1974 *Dark Horse* tour and album release.

George was intensely private and spiritual. He was devoted to meditation, chanting and the Hare Krishna movement. George had another side to him as well. He was charming, possessed a great wit and enjoyed being around people he considered friends. George had an old-fashioned streak because whenever the group was together, the men would be in one room and women would be in another. The men were inevitably creating music while Pattie and the ladies were preparing meals, dyeing each other's hair or sharing clothes. George and Ringo loved to have the women with them when we went out for dinner, events and parties.

George visited his former bandmate at the NBC studios in Burbank, California in February 1978 for the taping of "Ringo." The show was an hour-long television special loosely based on *The Prince and the Pauper* and intended to promote Ringo's *Bad Boy* album. George's visit was a major coup for the show and prompted a closed set with just a skeleton crew to film his part. However, I was able to snap away. George looked quite handsome in his Saville Row suit, and I joked that I had never seen him in a suit before. He smiled back and said, "I've got a couple of suits, Nancy."

The last time I saw George was when Ringo and I visited him and his second wife, Olivia Arias, at their Friar Park home, situated in Henley-on-Thames, England. Their house was filled with fresh flowers, burning incense, pictures of holy men and the smell of vegetarian Indian dishes wafting from the kitchen. He was so animated and happy, showing us through the house, or should I say castle. We had so much fun that night. He even took us through the cave under Friar Park with candles to show our way. We all piled into a small boat and George navigated through the dark canals until the stream opened up under low hanging trees in the garden. There was a peaceful playfulness that surrounded him and Olivia. It warms my heart when two people find each other and embrace happiness. They soon had a son, Dhani, who became the light in their lives.

After dinner we followed George up to his meditation room, his inner sanctum. At one point he and Ringo stopped chatting. Then George looked at me and said, "Nancy, I want to give you something." He took out a bowl of Indian cabochon blood rubies and told me to take as many as I wanted and design something for myself. I was astounded and asked for paper and pencil. I plopped down in front of the fireplace and started sorting through the rubies. Some were small and others ranged to the size of quail eggs. As George strummed the guitar and chatted with Ringo, I feverishly drew a design and showed it to the boys. He smiled and looked at Ringo and said, "Alright, I've given Nancy the stones, now you can give her the gold."

We later took the rubies and the design into London Asprey's and Ringo informed me they were the royal jeweler to the Queen. This little ol' girl from Alabama by way of New Jersey was going to have a necklace made by the Queen of England's jewelers!

Thank you, George...and Ringo.

Hare Krishna, George. Hare Krishna.

Pages 34-37: This series of images were shot on the set of "Ringo," a 1978 TV special in which George, handsome in his suit, had a cameo.

Left: Ringo and George rehearsing for a scene.

Right: George looking at his reflection while in makeup.

Above: In the cave under Friar Park, George's home in England. There was very little light but I managed to get an image. They look like two little boys exploring.

Right: Taken at Grand Prix in Monte Carlo in 1977. I love his intensity.

1943~2001

Above: Taken by May Pang in 1974, John is sitting on a Palm Springs road. *Photo: May Pang*

John Lennon
1943~1980

Ringo Starr wasn't the first Beatle in my life – that place is held by John Lennon.

John and May Pang, his and Yoko's secretary, moved from New York to Los Angeles in the fall of 1973 and were looking for a place to stay. Lou Adler, my boss at the time, offered his palatial Beverly Hills home for a few months. Having a Beatle in residence was a notch on his belt and provided him with a lifetime of bragging rights.

Scribes and historians described this period as John's "Lost Weekend", but I saw nothing to bolster that claim. During this time when John was with May, who had become his companion, he was on a creative and productive streak. That eighteen-month period saw the creation of the albums *Rock 'n' Roll*, *Walls and Bridges* and *Pussycats* as well as collaborations with Ringo Starr, Harry Nilsson, Elton John and David Bowie. The man was busy and anything but lost.

The three of us spent a lot of time hanging out in the studio where John was recording *Rock 'n' Roll* with Phil Spector or listening to music at the Troubadour where Linda Ronstadt and the Eagles were regulars. He also enjoyed the eclectic offerings of Los Angeles. One evening we went to a Bruce Lee movie at midnight with Bob Dylan. John loved eating at funky Chinese restaurants downtown because the food was great or getting hot dogs at Pinks or waiting in line for a delicious burrito from a Mexican stand. There was an unspoken understanding that a camera was not part of the comfort zone when he was among friends. It was about sharing time creatively that John loved. Thus the reason why I had to borrow a treasured photo from May Pang for this book.

On the other hand, John understood more than any other artist I knew how to convey his message through the media. John possessed one of the quickest minds, had a great wit and a big heart. He was on a higher metaphysical level than anyone I had ever met. If you wanted to be around John, you checked your "bullshit" at the door or be prepared to get caustically busted. It's no wonder that he and Harry Nilsson connected on so many levels, musically, politically and the heart. The *Pussycats* album was the ferment of these two great artists at that time...a classic.

John introduced me to one of the great loves of my life and for that I will be forever grateful. He thought Ringo and I would make a good couple, given some time. Time is relative, time is what it is and for however long it lasts you drink it up, drain the cup and smile. I think that's what John would say if he were here.

John Lennon came, he saw and he conquered, leaving marks on our souls, some deeper than others. It's extraordinary, but the night I got the phone call that John had died I was on my way out the door for some of that tasty Chinese food he so loved.

Ringo

I met Ringo Starr on Monday, May 27, 1974. John had rented actor Peter Lawford's Santa Monica beach home where he and May hosted many get-togethers. recording the *Pussycats* album. This party was to celebrate the birthday of Mal Evans, the Beatles' former roadie and good friend. John and May's gatherings meant friends, food, poker and a jam session at any given moment. Frequent guests included Keith Moon, Harry Nilsson, Jim Keltner, Jim Horn, Bobby Keyes, Danny Kootch, 'Sneaky' Pete Kleinow, Klaus Voorman, Jesse Ed Davis and Ringo's manager, Hilary Gerrard. Girlfriends and wives were cooking in the kitchen and kids were swimming in the pool. It was a family get-together, rock 'n' roll style.

A seat was offered to me at the poker table and I found myself next to Ringo. He was so charming, playful, witty and cute as hell. He might have had sad eyes, but they were twinkling at me that day. We flirted, oh how we flirted. At the time Ringo was estranged from his first wife Maureen and he was entangled with a friend of mine. So after I left the party, I put him out of my mind and off limits.

On August 6 I got a call from May, who announced she and John were back in town. They shuttled back and forth between New York and Los Angeles, so I kept their funky 1968 rust-colored Plymouth Barracuda in my garage. She asked me to bring the car to the Beverly Wilshire Hotel and we would hang out and have some dinner. I knocked on the door to the suite expecting to see John or May, but Ringo answered instead. It took me by surprise and I said, "Oh, hello." Ringo smiled and said, "I remember you...you're my poker partner."

The world's most famous drummer was riding high. His *Ringo* album had just been certified gold and spawned two No. 1 hits – "You're Sixteen" and "Photograph" as well as a Top 5 song, "Oh My, My." We all piled into the Barracuda and headed down to Sunset Sound Studios where Ringo was working on his album, *Goodnight Vienna*. John, May and I spent hours encouraging Ringo as he laid down vocals. When he finished we ventured to The Fiddler, a favorite hangout on Sunset and LaBrea that stayed open late and served delicious fried fish and chips. It had an old Wurlitzer jukebox loaded with an eclectic mix of songs. The two boys drank, dropped quarters in the jukebox, singing and discussing women, wives and life while May and I chatted, watching them.

Ringo turned more melancholy as the night drew to a close, holding my hand, touching my face, and looking at me with those big blue watery eyes. He weaved his way to the jukebox and punched in Charlie Rich's "The Most Beautiful Girl In The World" over and over again. At one point he was on his knees, resting his head against the speaker, which was at the bottom of the Wurlitzer.

"That poor guy," I said to John and May. "He's still in love with his wife. Look at him, his heart is broken." John was like E.F. Hutton. When he spoke, you listened. John said softly, "Nancy, he's a good lad... give him a chance."

At that moment I didn't realize just how prophetic John's statement would be.

Left: Taken in our garden in Los Angeles for promotion of the *Ringo the 4th* album.

This page: Bongo playing in the afternoon.

This page: Ringo was always a willing subject
when I was setting up my lights...what a sexy look!

Left: And then there is the other side of Ringo...not sure what the glove means but it works, giving this shot the silly factor.

Above: Soft light from a wall sconce set the tone for this mood.

England

Even though Ringo owned several residences around the globe and earned a reputation as part of the jet-set crowd, England was always his home.

Our trips to his native country were about reconnecting with what was important to Ringo – his family, his business dealings and his past. Ringo was a dyed-in-the-wool Brit. Wherever we were, we always had a pot of tea ready, Marmite in the cupboard, beans for toast and biscuits for dunking at tea time. Fish and chips, chicken and chips and chips and chips!

Ringo had business to tend to with his record and furniture design companies while in London. When he was asked by controversial filmmaker Ken Russell to play the part of the Pope in *Lisztomania* in February 1975, he jumped at the chance to spend a month in England. The movie was shot at Shepperton Studios in Middlesex. As is usually the case on a movie set, actors experience lots of down time while the camera crew spend an inordinate amount of time setting up lighting. It was during one of those down periods when I took my most famous shot of Ringo. Adjoining his dressing room was a bathroom with an enormous tub. The light that came through the long window above it was excellent. Ringo jumped in and feigned sleep… again, he was brilliant in front of the camera.

The heart of our visits was to spend time with his three children – sons Zak and Jason and daughter Lee. They were wonderful kids and adored their father, who doted on them in return. Ringo was very much a hands-on father. At home we played cards, worked on puzzles and cooked everyone's favorite meals. We also spent time at the movies, in museums and took day trips in the country. It was all very family-oriented.

On my first visit to England, Ringo was eager to show me London. That included a trip to the Tower of London where the Crown Jewels were on display, Buckingham Palace and a walk along the river Thames. I found the park benches along the Thames fascinating because they were so large with smooth beautiful swans for arm rests. I couldn't help thinking about all the people who had enjoyed their time sitting, watching the river. We were regular tourists when Ringo snapped a picture of me with Big Ben in the background. I asked him to sit on the bench. It was cold and windy that day so he stuffed his hands in his pockets and leaned his head back, acting as if he were asleep. I asked him what he was doing. He deadpanned without opening his eyes, "Ex-Beatle on the skids in London." The picture is pure Ringo and it never fails to make me smile.

On one of our trips to England, he took me to Liverpool to show me where it all started. Ringo became very nostalgic when he gave me a personalized tour of the city. Stops included 9 Madryn Street where Ringo was born in the front bedroom, the Royal Liverpool Children's Hospital where he was stricken with appendicitis just before his seventh birthday, the St. Silas School where he received his early education, and a stop at 10 Admiral Grove in the Dingle, the home where he lived from five to adulthood.

We also visited with his sweet and lovely mother, Elsie and his stepfather Harry, at their modest home in the community of Gateacre. I think I forever endeared myself to Elsie at dinner when I gorged on her roast potatoes. Elsie also taught me how to cook a delicious leg of lamb.

My introduction to England was beautiful because of Ringo and heartfelt because of the children. It will always have a special place in my heart.

Above: My first time in London.

Above: Ex-Beatle hits skid row.

Above: Exploring the shores of Devon with Jason, Zak and Lee.

Above: Ringo is a great father and storyteller.

Above: Me and Lee on a country lane.

Above: Father and son, Zak, having a quiet chat.

Above: Yum, fish 'n' chips at The Hunter's Inn, Devon.

Above: A few of Lee's small treasures were in this matchbox.

Left: Self portrait in the dressing room, Shepperton Studios.

Right: The Pope is dressed for his scene in *Lisztomania*, Shepperton Studios.

Left: Ringo is the master of using props, here a bathtub in his dressing room at Shepperton Studios.

Left: *Tommy* premiere in London.

Above: The Duke of Bedford's Rolls-Royce taking us to lunch at his estate.

Left & right: There was an antique dressing table with a three-sided mirror in our Ritz suite. We couldn't resist playing with the variations it offered for the camera.

Ritz Hotel beds with comfy down covers.

Los Angeles

By getting involved with one of the world's most famous musicians, it was as if I had stepped into another vortex. I explored strange new worlds, encountered all forms of alien life and did everything at warp speed. Less than six months after I met Ringo we were living together.

We stayed in the Beverly Wilshire Hotel for weeks at a time and soon, not having our own kitchen and privacy, Ringo and I wanted a home. One night we were invited to a dinner party at a fabulous house overlooking the city. I mentioned to the host that we were looking for a house just like this one. He said it was a furnished rental and was going to be available in two weeks. He put us in touch with the owner, Nicky Blair, who was a well-known Los Angeles restauranteur. We moved in and I began to set up house.

The 3,000-square-foot home was located off Sunset Plaza Drive and designed by architect Robert Byrd. It was a rambling cottage-style home that was perfect for us and our guests: four bedrooms, four baths, high vaulted ceilings, skylights and an amazing kitchen. The house faced a panoramic view of the city, and had special privacy landscaping, a small lemon tree grove and a sparkling swimming pool. Now my fun began… shopping for all the stuff a home needed…from the best sheets and towels to a stocked pantry.

It was an exciting, busy life, which included movie premieres, television cameos, award shows, night-clubbing, dinner parties and visiting friends. In the summers and at Christmas, Ringo's children – Zak, Jason and Lee – visited. They loved to explore, throw pool parties and visit Disneyland. Our home became a hub for our group of friends and family.

At the center of life in Los Angeles was Ringo's work. When he wasn't in the recording studio he was acting or making the promotional rounds for an album or film. Writing sessions, playing on friends albums, business dinners, barbeques, slide shows…these were all the creative things that made up our life at the time. He had also formed his own record label and furniture design company. We had a full schedule.

Los Angeles was a more closely-knit community back in the 1970s. There wasn't the celebrity feeding frenzy that exists today with the paparazzi. People were respectful of celebrities and didn't hound them. Other celebrities were more open to developing friendships and we enjoyed their company.

During that time so many of Ringo's friends were also working and living in Los Angeles so any given night there would be Harry Nilsson, Keith Moon, Dr. John or Jim Keltner sitting round the living room sharing and preparing music to be recorded.

Our home was a safe haven where we could enjoy our family and friends, retain a sense of privacy and work in the most exciting industry in the world. More importantly, our home was filled with love and creativity.

Left: Carly Simon at our house after lunch with Ringo and Arif Mardin.

Above: Ringo and Vini Poncia, his friend and writing partner on several albums.

Left & above: Actor Jon Voight
and his adorable daughter, Angelina,
enjoying our pool at a birthday party
for Jason Starkey.

Left & above: Lee Starkey in her pretty party dress.

Left: Paparazzi outside of Mr. Chow's, Beverly Hills.
Above: Our European alter egos.

Left - clockwise: Mentor Williams and Tom Jans. Tom Jans giving me a guitar. Seymour Cassell and Chi Coltran. Klaus Voorman. Everyone was there to help celebrate my birthday in Los Angeles in 1975.

Above - clockwise: Olivia and George Harrison, Cynthia and Klaus Voorman. George Harrison, Jim Keltner and me. Harry Nilsson and Mac Rebennack. Harry Nilsson.

Left: At a friend's house.

Above: At Disneyland, sporting our fabulous hats we bought on Main Street.

Above: Hilary Gerrard having a 'cuppa tea' and being a good sport while I fiddled with my lights.

Right: The man turns thirty-five!

Above: Fun pictures taken backstage at a Christmas charity concert in Los Angeles.

Left: Another airport.

Above: Attending the premiere of *The Late Show* in Westwood, California.

Don't Forget: "KLAATU BARADA NIKTO"

Left: A promotion sticker for the album, *Goodnight Vienna*.

Above: Getting Ringo ready for the video.

Right: Ringo marching at Hollywood and Vine in front of the Capitol Records building, Los Angeles.

Left: Lee Starkey couldn't leave the table until she finished her peas. I would sneak by and eat some to help her out, Los Angeles.

Above: Father and daughter in Monte Carlo. Are they cute or what?

Above: With Lee, Jason and Zak, Los Angeles, 1977.

Right: Zak on drums. There was always a kit set up and he had the best teachers.

Left: My best friend Andee and her husband, Rick Nathanson, at the Miller Drive mansion. I love this photo, what can I say, they brought music and merriment wherever they went.

Above: We were always making our own fairy tales with our friends on 16mm film. Lee is a true fairy, and a good little actress.

Above: Dressed as the princess, my fairy companion led me to the magic room.

Above: Ringo playing the mad monk in our homemade fairy tale.

Above: Nancy with her Scottish warlord?

Below: Percy arrives at Miller Drive.

Left: The light was beautiful on the balcony of our room facing the ocean in Maui, Hawaii, 1975.

Above: Ringo not happy with the chips served.

Left: *Photo: Andee Nathanson.*

Above: This was a fun day enjoyed with our friends, Andee and Rick Nathanson at the cavernous mansion on Miller Drive in Los Angeles. We made music, took photos of each other and ate delicious food.

Pattie Boyd

Pattie Boyd's natural beauty, matched by her inner loveliness, has inspired some of the greatest love songs of our time, earning her a legendary status as rock's best-known muse.

Like her two very famous ex-husbands – George Harrison and Eric Clapton – Pattie is British to the core. She's polite, proper, modest and sweet. Always ready with a smile or to give a compliment, Pattie is one of the most generous souls I've ever known.

Pattie's generosity was evident the first time I met her in August 1971. My boyfriend, Carl Radle and I arrived in New York City just in time for *The Concert for Bangla Desh* soundcheck and I didn't have any fresh clothes to wear. Pattie brought me back to their hotel suite and laid out her best clothes and encouraged me to pick anything. That selfless act of kindness bonded us immediately.

We developed a wonderful friendship, so when she and George came to Los Angeles in 1973 to promote *Living in the Material World* we met often. One day Pattie dressed me up and took some wonderful pictures of me lounging on the trees in the garden of their rented Bel Air home. She has a natural eye for photography and both of us having been models, well...dressing up is what we love to do!

I remember around this time Led Zeppelin was in town, staying at the Continental Hyatt House on the Sunset Strip. When I arrived she told me of a party at the "Riot House" and said we should go. The group occupied the entire top floor and the scene was textbook '70s rock 'n' roll. Stepping off the elevator, we were grazed by a man on a motorcycle doing a wheelie, who must have been going at 30 mph because his screeching brakes ripped up the carpet as his wheels bounced off the wall at the end of the hallway. Pattie and I looked at each other and laughed, knowing we had stepped into another world. All of the doors were open, music was blaring and people were passing joints and drinking God knows what from plastic cups. As we cruised down the smoky hallway we peeked into each room, looking for a familiar face. Zeppelin's drummer John Bonham, came running out of a room carrying a TV and invited us to watch him throw it at a Cadillac convertible a dozen stories below parked in front of the hotel. Someone had bet him a thousand dollars he couldn't land the TV in the backseat. Pattie and I craned out the adjoining window to watch. As "Bonzo", his nickname and rightfully given, mulled over his calculations I noticed that there was another TV in the bushes next to the Caddy. Bonham launched the large Panasonic and we all watched as it landed square in the back seat and promptly bounced out and onto the trunk with a crash. Everybody in the room screamed with delight. When questioned whose car he destroyed, Bonham said he had no idea. With the sound of sirens and sensing the police were probably on their way, Pattie said in her sweet, inimitable way, "Perhaps we should go now. Thank you John for a lovely time."

As friends sometimes do, we lost touch. I hadn't seen Pattie for nearly three decades when in September 2007 I flew to New York to show my support at Pattie's book signing and the gallery opening of her photographs. The next week her book, *Wonderful Tonight* hit the top of *The New York Times*' best-seller list. We picked up where we left off and shared a quiet moment together talking about our families and photography. "Pattie, it's now time for the girls," I said. She looked at me and gave me that adorable smile, "Yes it is, isn't it?"

Left & right: Girls can't help playing dress-up, especially when there is a great photographer to take your picture.
Photos: Pattie Boyd

New York City

New York and Los Angeles are not only separated by about 3,000 miles, but each city has its own energy that flows through anyone who visits. New York is both cosmopolitan and gritty while Los Angeles is notoriously laid back and all about image. Despite the hustle and bustle, Ringo found out that the Big Apple was conducive for making music. While Los Angeles might have been the music capital of the world at the time, Manhattan had a tempo that gave him a new power to express himself.

On January 9, 1977, we flew to New York so that Ringo could record *Ringo the 4th*. Veteran producer Arif Mardin, who recorded hits for the Bee Gees, Aretha Franklin, The Average White Band, Phil Collins and Hall & Oates, was overseeing the project. The album was a different direction for Ringo, who rolled up his sleeves and went to work.

While he was digging in at the studio I was enjoying my old hometown. I visited with relatives, caught up with old friends and set aside some time for a little retail therapy. We set up home and headquarters for the next three weeks in the world famous Plaza Hotel. The suite boasted a spectacular view of Central Park. While we were there a blizzard had blanketed the entire city with a couple feet of snow. All modes of transportation ground to a halt for a few days, the city was quiet and still as we watched people playing and cross-country skiing through the park.

I guess it was about that time that we were talking about the title of the album, *Ringo the 4th*, when Ringo said, "It sounds so medieval." Immediately, his eyes lit up. "I want a sword," he announced

My old friend, Kathy Dorritie, otherwise known to the world as "Cherry Vanilla", knew of a place that rented props where we found a fabulous sword. There was a huge walk-in closet in our suite at the Plaza that was perfect for the shoot. Ringo and I thought bouncing light would create a great look. My girlfriend from Tulsa, Rita Wolf, was the model who sat on his shoulders on the album cover. She had flown in a few days before the storm to visit us. We weren't sure if the shots would work but we had a ball dressing up Ringo and sitting him on a waste paper bin with a pillow on top. For the back of the album Ringo and Rita just turned around and I shot their backs…it was brilliant. *Ringo the 4th* was my first album cover credit.

We returned to New York in late April for the spring release of the album. The next day we were strolling down Fifth Avenue when we literally bumped into Paul and Linda McCartney. There was a photographer following them and snapped us all together.

We also visited John and Yoko in their apartment in the Dakota one afternoon and met little toddler Sean. John was as happy as I'd ever seen him. Ever since Sean's birth, John seemed to be at peace. He was baking bread, holding his son and enjoying his long break from the music business. It was all about the baby, sharing recipes and his home life. On another visit we all went to eat at a Chinese restaurant. It was not a fancy restaurant, but the food was great. Very John.

For John's thirty-sixth birthday, Ringo and I asked Cherry Vanilla to deliver a special performance of her very racy rendition of *Romeo and Juliet*. John called afterward to tell us that it was his favorite interpretation of William Shakespeare's work!

Central Park from our hotel suite at the Plaza after the 1977 snow storm.

Above left: Cherry outside the Dakota after delivering a birthday poem to John.

Above right: Cherry with flowers that Ringo and I sent in return.

Left: Cherry visiting the Atlantic studios while *Ringo the 4th* was being recorded.

Right: Gorgeous Rita Wolf, the legs on the *Ringo the 4th* album cover.

Above: Engineer Lew Hahn and Arif Mardin discussing the mix as Ringo listens to the playback.

Above: Me, Ringo, Linda and Paul caught strolling down Fifth Avenue. *Photo: Corbis*

Above: Ringo and Arif in our living room.

Left: Arif and Lew Hahn, his engineer, at Atlantic Studios, New York City.

Above: Ringo and Vini Poncia, Ringo's collaborator on *Ringo the 4th*, in the lobby of the Plaza Hotel after a night in the studio, New York City.

Right: Arif checking his notes.

Keith Moon

Keith Moon had a continuous movie playing inside his head, and the rest of the world unwittingly became his supporting cast.

Every time I saw Keith, it seemed as if he was in character. I remember once Ringo and I went to his house for a party and he answered the door dressed as a pirate. Not only was he dressed for the part, but like a good method actor, he responded to everyone as if he was in *Treasure Island*.

"Yeoman Lassee, what can I fix you to drink, matey?" he'd say, then add, "arrggghh" at the end of every sentence. He was a riot. Once again, I was the lucky girl with my trusty SX-70 Polaroid camera.

Keith had a serious side, too, and it didn't matter what state of mind he was in, he was right there with you. He looked at me with those big black eyes with so much compassion and he really listened to what I had to say. We connected on a very basic family level and he knew that I adored him. The adoration was mutual because he felt that I truly loved Ringo and wasn't there for my own gain. He showed me such respect and treated me like I was the lady of the house.

Sometime in August 1977 Ringo and I visited him at his Trancas Beach home in Malibu. This time, we encountered what I call, "The Great Philosopher." Keith had cut a hole in a sheet, wrapped a rope around his waist and there was an instant toga! He rounded out the costume with a goblet of wine and a large book, made grand gestures with his hands and espoused philosophy on life.

His interaction with Ringo was incredibly intimate. I've noticed over the years that drummers have a shorthand language and they don't need complete sentences to convey their thoughts. Ringo and Keith could say two or three words to each other and there would be an instant understanding.

That particular day at the beach Ringo and I brought his kids to see Keith. We sat on blankets, made sandcastles, ate sandwiches and caught up with each other's lives. After a while, Keith and I took a walk down the beach, away from the group. As always, I brought my camera with me. He was talking about how much he loved the ocean and turned around and looked at me. I already had the camera up to my face and I took a picture. Looking back, I can't for the life of me remember what he was specifically saying but the result was an unguarded moment. In most of my pictures, he's either laughing, putting on a show or taking on a different persona. But that beautiful picture where I peeped into his soul for just a second is my favorite photo of him.

Keith was all about friendship and his big lion heart. He was on loan to earth for thirty-two years and then it was time for him to go.

Above: At a party at Keith's house.

Right: Ringo and Keith on the beach with Dougal Butler, Keith's friend and right hand man.

Far right: Pirate Moon.

These pages: A day at the beach with Keith, Ringo and Zak Starkey.

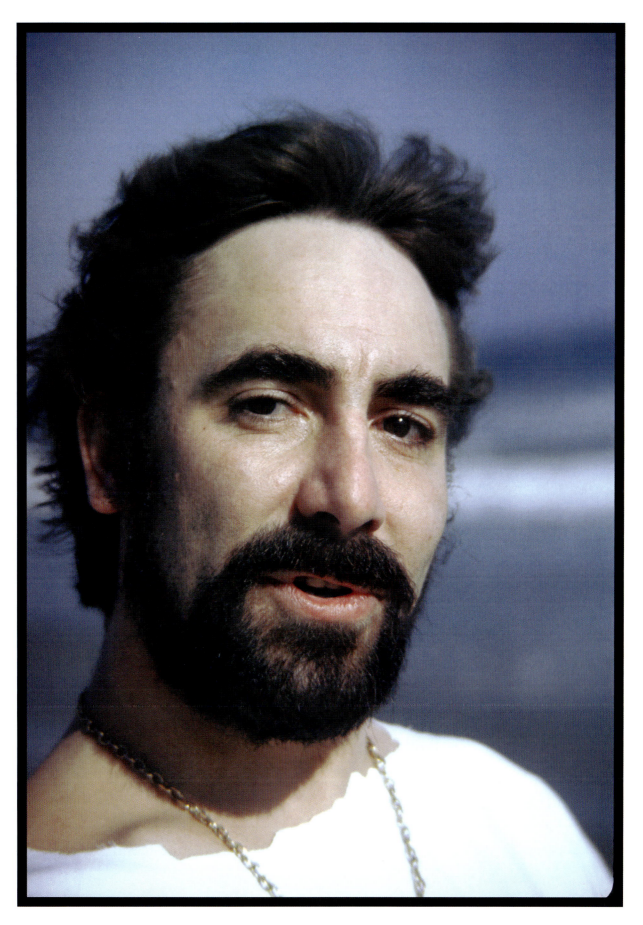

1947-1978

Harry Nilsson

If Harry Nilsson was a relative of mine, he would have been my favorite cousin.

I've met some fun and interesting people in my years, but Harry was perhaps one of the most brilliant. The two-time Grammy winner was a force of nature, an iconoclast, a savant, a manic-genius. He was well-versed in world politics, past and present, built a home in honor of the artist M.C. Escher and could perform complex mathematical equations in his head. If you gave him your birth date, he could tell you what day you were born. He was spot-on every time.

Harry was that way with his life, too. Everything was right there up front and center, open doorways as he navigated through a conversation from one topic to the next, all meshing together. He had his music life, his movie life, his home life and his party life. Harry did the latter in spades. He could out-drink, out-smoke and out-snort all of his contemporaries, creating an edge that was Olympic. After an all-night gathering, everybody would either go home, sleep where they sat or crash on the floor. Not Harry. Often I'd find him in my living room in the wee hours of the morning smoking a cigarette, pushing the buttons on the cable box searching for news, catching up on the world.

He was a brilliant songwriter because he had a remarkable ear and a wry sense of humor, which is so prevalent in his songs. His voice is legendary, haunting. Harry was the kind of guy who could walk into a bar and know everyone's life story by the end of the evening. One night Ringo and I walked into a Sunset Boulevard bar with Harry, who upon entering, rolled up a $50 bill and told the piano player, "This is for *not* playing 'Feelings' while we're here."

The last time I saw Harry was in the mid-'80s and he couldn't stop hugging me. He was a big Teddy Bear and the most loyal friend anyone could have. He had such a huge heart, which finally gave out when he was only fifty-two years old.

I loved Harry then and I miss him now.

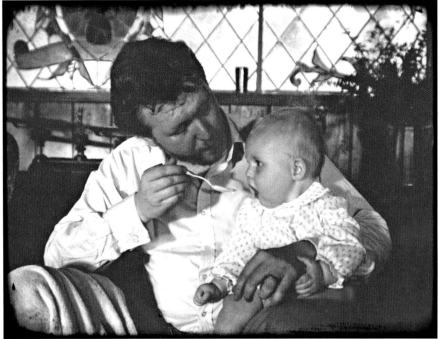

Left: Harry and his first son, Beau, were so sweet to watch. He was a great father.

Above right: Harry and his wife Una at my house in Los Angeles before I moved in with Ringo. They lived with me for a few months until they found a place of their own, 1974.

Below right: Harry on the lawn at a garden party at our Haslem Terrace home, Hollywood Hills, 1975.

1941-1994

Tom Jans

Whenever I think of Tom Jans, three things come to mind: cowboy boots, classic literature and poetry.

"Tommy" was a ranch boy from San Luis Obispo and he looked every bit the part – blonde wavy hair, caramel-colored eyes, suede ranch jackets, blue jeans and cowboy boots.

He was my next door neighbor when I first moved to Los Angeles in 1972. We both worked on the A&M lot and lived in the fabulous English Tudor-style apartments high up in the Hollywood hills, built by Columbia Studios in the 1920s. We became instant friends and he was like my brother and I think I was the sister he never had.

Tommy was riding high on his huge hit "Lovin' Arms," making him one of the hottest writers in Los Angeles at the time. He was hugely respected by the record industry, and for good reason: Tommy's songwriting was rich. Elvis Presley, Frank Sinatra, Kris Kristofferson, Rita Coolidge, Bette Midler and Etta James were but a few stars who recorded Tommy's songs.

Whenever I popped into Tommy's apartment, he would make us a cup of tea with half and half and sage honey. He was usually reading poetry or deep into something like Lord Byron and always a guitar an arm's reach away. Nobody in Los Angeles read Lord Byron.

A late-life baby and an only child, Tommy possessed a razor sharp wit and a fun-loving personality. He was warm, sensitive and like most writers, had a wonderful sense of humor. He was a total clown and made no qualms about making a fool of himself. Tommy is one of the few people I have met who didn't have a mean bone in his body.

Women were crazy about Tommy because he was such a sexy man. Every girlfriend I ever had fell in love with Tommy, including my little sister. He broke all of their hearts. I was lucky enough to catch Tommy's sexiness on film when I took shots for his 1982 album, *Champion.* There was a connection between the two of us as well as the beautiful girl he was posing with, my friend Garrie Kelly. She was in love with him, too!

Tommy wrote a poem for me called *Mother's Eyes* that inspired a song on the *Champion* album. That song came out of a long evening in front of a raging fire and some Chateauneuf du Pape talking about family and mothers. I lost my mother when she was thirty-one and I was just thirteen. When he sang it to me, it turned the key to my heart. He managed to capture the essence of my pain. Later, for my birthday, he gave me the Yamaha guitar used for the song's composition.

As I have experienced firsthand with most artists, Tommy had a deep, dark place that he entered at times. He struggled with depression and occasionally would break down. During those periods he would come to me and have me hold him. It wasn't anything sexual, but just a soft place where he could lay his head and rest. One night he confessed, "I will always, always love you. I will carry that to my grave." We both cried.

Not long after he spoke those words Tommy died from organ failure from injuries sustained in a 1984 motorcycle accident. He was thirty-six.

I have always thought of Tommy as my angel – an angel with muddy feet.

Above: We shot this late one night in an old 1940s Pontiac. We wanted the windows black and the interior to look better than it really was.

Above: Garrie Kelly looks so beautiful over Tom's shoulder. I think they were crazy about each other.

Left: Tom had a vision in his head for his album cover. The title at the time was *Workin' Hot*. I think this image conveys the edge he was searching for in his music.

1948–1984

Actress and equestrian,
Mary Louise Weller, Los Angeles.

142

The Ladies

Rock 'n' roll has always been and forever will be a boy's club, but within that club exists a silent but strong sisterhood.

I have been fortunate in my lifetime to befriend the large cross section of ladies in this book. They've included singers, actresses, photographers, writers, models, muses, housewives, girlfriends and significant others. Our first common link is music. Our second common link is men.

Women are definitely the most fascinating subjects to photograph. They play to the camera and fall into a seductive personality. Each image of the women in this chapter is unique. Some are captured just being themselves while others are in situations I created to heighten the feminine magnetism of the subject.

With women I can share my vision and together we can bring it to life on film. Perhaps it goes back to playing dress-up as little girls, creating our imaginary worlds in which we are special and beautiful.

Right: Friend and fellow photographer Andee Nathanson hugging a tree in the yard of our new house up in the Hollywood Hills. The house had belonged to Mama Cass from the Mamas and the Papas, so it had a history.

Above left: Shelley Duvall, South of France 1978.

Above right: Rita Coolidge, 1971.

Above far right: Annette Walter-Lax was Keith Moon's girlfriend from Germany. A beauty at his beach house in Malibu.

Right: Carol Paulus, hairdresser to the stars and a good friend to me and Ringo. She also played her part in our fairy tales.

MRS. PASUCO HOLDS PHOTO OF RINGO, GRANDDAUGHTER
(DAILY Photo by Jeff Field)

Future Mrs. Ringo Starr's grandmother lives here

By CATHY D. WAHL
DAILY Staff Writer

Flowers wired from Los Angeles came to Mrs. Estelle Pasuco of Decatur Wednesday in honor of her 72nd birthday. The card was signed "Richard" for Richard Starkey, Mrs. Pasuco's prospective grandson-in-law.

As most people under 35 know, Richard Starkey is Ringo Starr's real name.

How did a Decatur woman come to be Ringo's future grandmother in-law? A beautiful granddaughter, Nancy Andrews, comes into the picture.

Miss Andrews, a model, first met Ringo Starr when she went to Los Angeles to work. A native of Jersey City, N.J., Miss Andrews' first modeling assignments came in nearby New York.

Although Mrs. Pasuco was born and reared in Decatur, she lived with her family for more than 30 years in New

Left: My grandmother in Decatur, Alabama, was so happy when she heard I was engaged to be married.

Right: My sister, Jennarae. I had to bat the men off her. They didn't seem to mind that she was only 17!

Right: Jenny Anderson, a great writer and actress. This British beauty had just finalized her divorce from Jethro Tull flute player Ian Anderson. Jenny wrote the lyrics to his famous hit, "Aqualung".

Left: Kim Carnes and I had just finished lunch after a publicity shoot. She was riding high on "Betty Davis Eyes".

Right: An outtake from a shoot for a nutrition book by Katharine Ross. A woman with a great sense of humor.

Above: A great singer and a friend to this day, Duitch Helmer and her macaw.

Left: Helena Kallianiotes, an actress with a big heart. She had a classy dance club in Silver Lake, Los Angeles.

Right: The one and only May Pang. Her beauty shines even brighter today. Palm Springs, 1974 (archive of May Pang).

Above left: Kiki Dee and me on a barge in Amsterdam. Ringo and I were there with all of Elton John's friends for a concert and party, 1975.

Below left: Phoebe Snow playing a hand game with Chris O'Dell. Jenny Anderson gives me a smile. We were backstage at a Leon Russell concert in Los Angeles, 1974.

Above right: Phoebe at the birthday party that Ringo gave me in Los Angeles, 1975.

Below right: Phoebe came up to the house to show me the cover of *Rolling Stone*. She was on the cover. "Poetry Man" was a huge smash for her.

Left: Susin S. Fair has been my friend since 1967. We were young models in New York City while going to school. Ringo, his good friend and business manager – Hilary Gerrard, Susin and I had a crazy but memorable vacation in the Yucatan in 1977. She's one of the sexiest women with brains on the planet.

Right: Andee Nathanson at William Royere's memorial on Donovan's ranch in Joshua Tree, California. She is my soul sister and has been an important part of my life. We share photography and secrets like others share recipes. We give creative support to each other on many levels. She was an anchor to Ringo and me.

Left: Aya Tarlow is a unique artist who inspired all of us to be creative. She and her husband William Royere's home was a hub for us to gather and share.

Right: Dolly Parton signing the wall of autographs at record producer, Ken Mansfield's house. Ringo loved country music and was in heaven that night.

Above: Shelley Long between trailers in Durango, Mexico on the set of *Caveman*. I remember her as a beautiful and funny woman.

Right: Cathy Cyphers Soref was the best addition to my life in 1979. A true friend who has given love and support unconditionally all these years. Today she is a philanthropist and the founder of DNA Stuff, a non-profit organization that raises funds for basic genetic research at Cold Spring Harbor, New York.

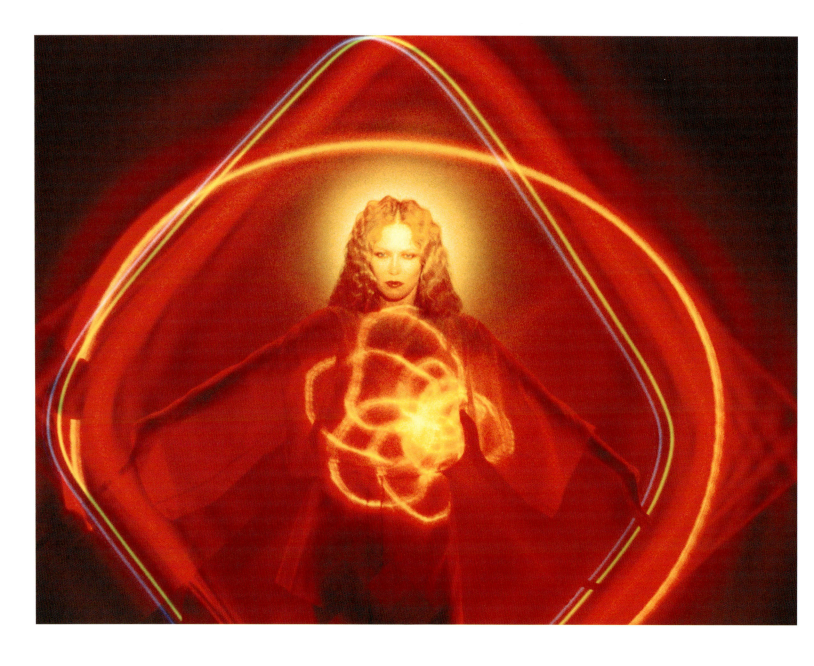

Above: The gorgeous Garrie Kelly. I had this idea to photograph lasers, merging them with beauty and fashion. She helped me nail it. They turned out to be very spiritual and other-worldly.

Right: Mary Kenny was a great friend to me and Ringo. She could handle any situation. A girl that understood the music business.

Left: Me after ballet class at
the Miller Drive mansion.

Above: What can I say?
Anyone for badminton?

Wild and crazy (like a fox) Mel Brooks. My friend, Susin S. Fair interviewed him for a New York Sunday magazine and I took the photos. What a fun man!

The Gentlemen

There's an old saying that the difference between a good photographer and a great one is access. Because of my relationship with Ringo Starr, I was offered a front row seat to the show and given a backstage pass to a world behind the velvet rope.

I met with captains of industry to *Captain Fantastic*. I partied with royalty and disco queens, dined at tables set with gold and eaten on paper plates with the rich and famous. It gets down to one thing they all have in common – they are just like you and me. The same things matter in their lives: family, food, shelter and happiness.

It's no secret among celebrities that there exists a social hierarchy. At the very top rung of the ladder were the Beatles. Actors, aristocracy, tycoons and musicians all wanted to meet Ringo Starr. This unfettered access allowed me to meet a lot of interesting people and forge strong friendships over the years.

As a former tomboy, I befriended many famous men. I believe they sensed I had no ulterior motives and didn't want anything from them. I treated everyone like extended family and that comfort led to unguarded moments caught by my lens.

I've realized over the years that men are different to photograph than women. Most just want you to take the picture and be done with it, while others will flirt and pose but the majority are usually themselves with no pretense. I like to coax them into a mood and make a connection, giving them a comfort zone.

The images in this chapter cover a gamut of situations. Some are professional set ups but most are candid. There are images where the quality is not so pristine but the moments captured convey their personalities.

Left: Time spent with the brilliant Terry Southern was like being with a big, cuddly teddy bear who loved food, friends and women and diverse, exciting conversation. Terry wrote and contributed to some of the greatest screenplays of our time: *Dr. Strangelove, The Magic Christian, The Cincinnati Kid, Casino Royale, Barbarella* and *Easy Rider*, to name a few. *Photo: Andee Nathanson.*

Left & right: Gregg Allman
taken at the Silverdome, 1987.

Above & right: Duane Allman was on our plane and he had a sense of humor because the bottle of wine was empty. In the shot opposite he really is asleep.

1948~1971

Left: Carl Perkins, the artist who gave us "Blue Suede Shoes".

Right: Eric Clapton in Connecticut, 1974.

Left: Mac Rebennack, otherwise known as 'Dr. John the Night Tripper'. On this day he was a daddy at a children's birthday party at our house in Los Angeles.

Above: Keyboard player David Foster, later to be a famous producer, taken backstage in Hollywood at a charity event in 1976.

Left: Edgar Winter on
stage in Russia in 1987.

Above: Billy Vera,
Hollywood, 1979.

Above left: Hoyt
Axton, Arlo Guthrie,
Jennarae Andrews and
Jackie Guthrie on a flight
from Tulsa to Los Angeles
in 1976. Hoyt played the
guitar and the entire first
class sang along. Doubt if
it would happen today.

Left: Jackie and
Arlo Guthrie.

Right: Hoyt in 1989
at the Palomino Club
parking lot in the San
Fernando Valley. We were
at a motorcycle rally to
collect Toys For Tots.

Left: Actor Seymour Cassell on the set of "Ringo".

Right: Monty Python's Eric Idle in the South of France 1977.

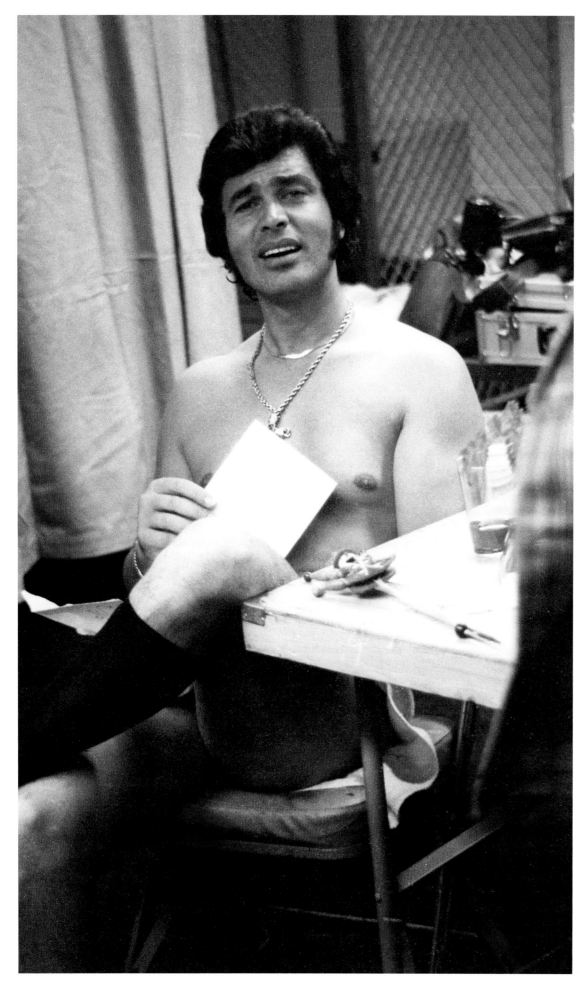

Left: Engelbert Humperdinck backstage at a Christmas charity show. He didn't mind me taking this photo of him in his underwear reading a fan letter.

Right: Sonny Bono was at the same Christmas charity show. Love the Elvis jumpsuit!

Left: Jeff Baxter, better known as 'Skunk', the amazing guitarist with the Doobie Brothers.

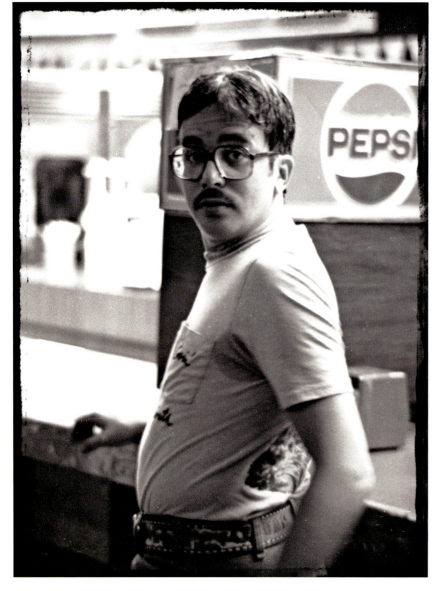

Top left: Producer Ken Mansfield and concert promoter Alan Pariser.

Top right: Glen Campbell.

Left: Van Dyke Parks, genius composer.

Above: Steve Gadd, drummer extraordinaire, Los Angeles.

Right: The one and only Steve Cropper, guitar player and songwriter.

Left: Producer, writer, performer, and mystery man, Tom Slocum.

Above: Two photos of William Royere. A director, a mentor and an astrologer to the stars.

Right: Singer Tommy Steele showed us around when Ringo and I were on holiday in Spain 1978.

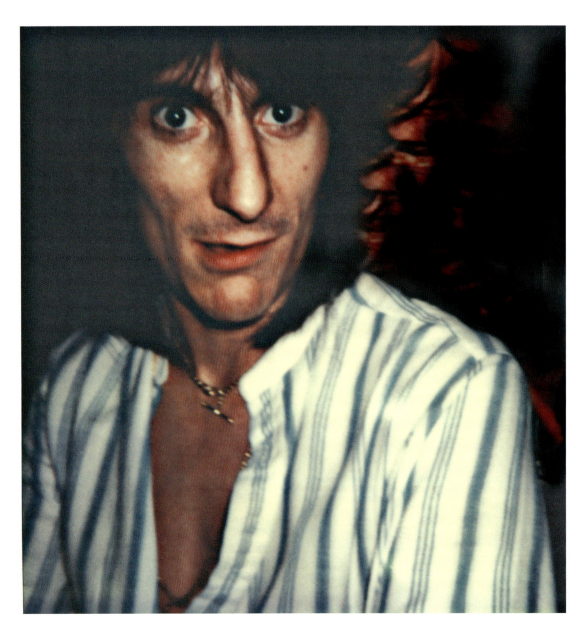

Above: Ronnie Wood was surprised when I
shot this Polaroid of him. Hollywood, 1979.

Above: Johnny Rivers at Knotts Berry Farm where he was performing a concert in 1976.

Left: Richard Beymer, that heartthrob "Tony" in *Westside Story*. A talented actor and friend.

Right: John Badham directed *Dracula* and I took this of him in a mirror with some silly glasses on.

Monte Carlo

Monte Carlo has long been known for its glamor, royalty, casinos, movie stars, aristocrats, shipping magnates...the playground for the rich and famous. But it was more of a refuge for Ringo and me when we needed to take a break and unwind.

We moved to Monte Carlo in the summer of 1976. The main reason Ringo moved there was to become an alien resident and take advantage of Monaco's favorable tax laws. That's pretty funny when I think about it because it's the most expensive real estate in the world and not much bigger than Central Park.

Ringo and I lived in a spacious three-bedroom apartment on the thirty-third floor overlooking the Mediterranean Sea. It was a very relaxed lifestyle that consisted of reading, writing music, drives along the coast, cooking and fine dining. A couple of nights a week we'd walk to Costa Rica, our favorite restaurant, where I could get my fill of the best Bellinis and caviar.

When we felt like dressing up and going out, we'd go to the Loew's Casino where the croupiers were American and the gaming tables were full of Texans and junkets from the USA. We'd dance the night away at Regines, a classic 1970s disco. Owned by nightclub impresario Regine Zylberberg, the disco featured oak staircases, wrought-iron stools, marble countertops and shell-shaped toilet seats. And, oh yes, plenty of stars and Arabs.

My favorite time was in the fall when the little principality would become a town and the only people there would be the true residents. That's when I would roller skate on the promenade because there were so few people. The locals must have thought I was a crazy American girl.

Another form of entertainment was the Formula One Monaco Grand Prix, which was first staged in 1929. It was an insane time as the town shut down for days. The twisting 77-lap circuit was staged around the narrow, winding streets of Monte Carlo and up the twisting mountain roads. The sound of the racing cars blasting around hairpin turns had the crowds cheering. People could stand only a few yards away from the track. It was non-stop screaming engines, smoking tires, wall-to-wall people, and a thrilling race course that allowed no room for error. The race was a high-powered 'show and tell' of the world's elite.

George Harrison, a Formula One enthusiast, visited us in Monte Carlo in May 1977. Jackie Stewart, who competed in Formula One between 1965 and 1973 and won three world championships, was the race announcer for ABC's "Wide World of Sports". George's friendship with Jackie gave us an all-access pass, which started with a Thursday practice session preceding the Friday race. It boggled my mind to see the transition of this gorgeous place into a living, breathing racetrack but everyone was dressed in Gucci, Chanel or Cartier.

I tagged along with Ringo, George and Jackie. With my Nikon in hand, I was able to snap behind the scenes – from the Formula drivers to Regine Zylberberg's elite party held on her terrace overlooking one of the tightest turns in the race.

I visited Monte Carlo again in June 2007 for lunch with close friends. Sadly, I found it not to be the same town I remembered. There were so many tall buildings blocking the view of the majestic hills and the water. The Monte Carlo I recall is only preserved in my mind and in my photos.

Right: George Harrison with famous racing driver, Jackie Stewart and Ringo at the 1977 Monte Carlo Grand Prix.

Left: Ringo was an avid fiction reader.

Above: An afternoon on Spiro Niarchos' speedboat. Spiro is the son of Greek shipping magnate Stavros Niarchos.

Left: George and Jackie.

Right: Formula One racecar.

Below: Monte Carlo Casino taken from the Hotel de Paris.

Right: Taken on the balcony of our apartment overlooking Monte Carlo. It was used as the cover for the *Bad Boy* album.

Left & right: Out for a walk in Monte Carlo.

Left: The beautiful Mediterranean Sea is the backdrop for this silhouette.

Above: I just love photo booths.

Above: Nigel Dempster of the *Daily Mail* and disco queen, Regine.

Above: Michael and Pat York at a party during the Grand Prix.

Donovan

Even though Donovan Philips Leitch was born in Glasgow, Scotland in May 1946, I'm convinced he's a troubadour from the Emerald City from another time.

I first met Donovan in the mid-'70s at an afternoon garden party at William Royere's home in Los Angeles. William and his wife Aya were a creative couple who inspired all those around them and many artists gravitated to their home. Donovan was under a fruit tree holding court, singing one of his Scottish folklore songs on his guitar, turning adults into children and transporting those children to magical kingdoms. He loves the whole idea of creating art and having it evolve as music, film, poetry, literature or photos. It didn't matter as long as there was music and fairies and merriment.

From this wonderful salon evolved many unique projects directed and written by William. The one that was close to his and Donovan's heart was *Beetle Shrine*. It was an original fairy tale of a very old peddler who faces his mortality, and questions the moon, the trees and the water about his life. Through all this he befriends a small beetle who tenderly counsels him. Donovan and William put the production together and I assisted as well as took all the stills. It never saw the light of day because William Royere died before the film completed edit. We were all devastated because the loss was so enormous to our circle of friends.

As much as it sounds as if Donovan had his head in another world, he was surprisingly focused. He was able to change hats in the blink of an eye – a true chameleon. A photographer has to find a way to connect to the subject and tease that special essence out of them. Donovan loved connection, especially on a creative level. He was like a sly little boy with telling you, "I've got a secret and I just might tell you what it is." Well, I already knew what the secret was – *we're having fun and we're creating together*.

We had all read *The Mists of Avalon*, a famous novel by Marion Zimmer Bradley, in which she retells the Arthurian legends from a woman's perspective. It inspired us to do a shoot, magical, other-worldly and good. Donovan wore crowns, capes, and used musical instruments as props and quickly morphed into character. His beautiful wife, Linda became part of the event when she joined the session. Though he's a singer and songwriter by trade, Donovan is an incredible performer. He doesn't pose but becomes the character or whoever you need him to be. As a photographer, you have to keep up with him and keep your finger down on the shutter button.

Donovan was amazing because he never gave me the same look twice. The contact sheets I have of him show that every picture is different within its own frame. Usually a session garners a few good photos. With Donovan, it's a hard choice.

Above & right: Contacts from a shoot.
Donovan and his beautiful wife, Linda.

223

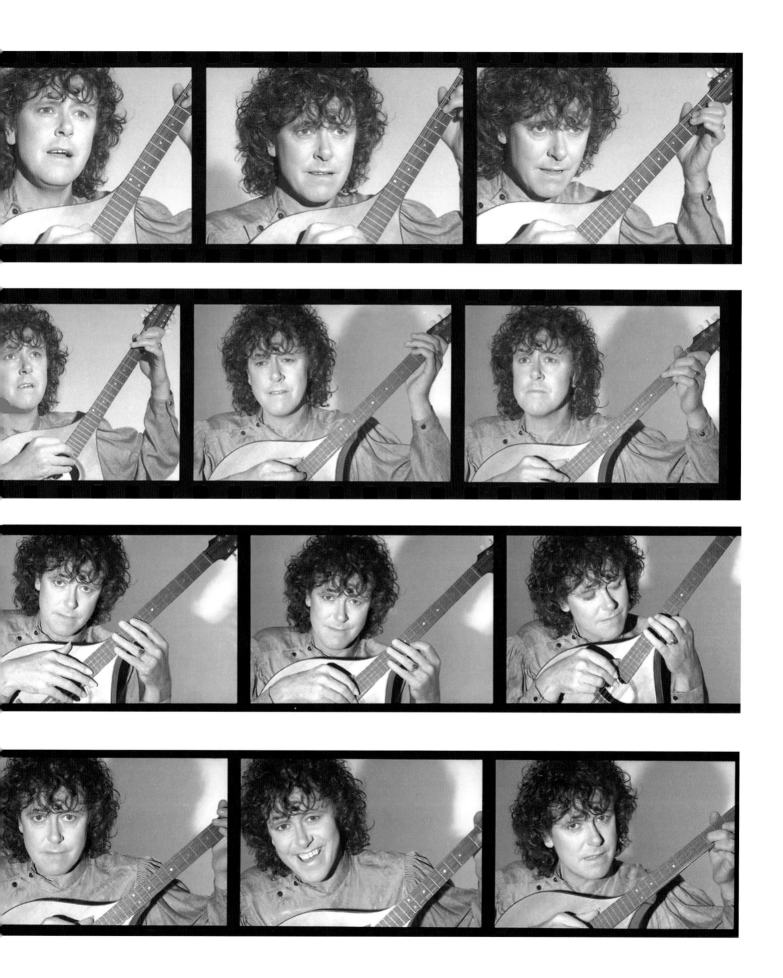

225

Donovan as the wise old
peddler in William Royere's
fairy tale, *Beetle Shrine*.

Bernie Taupin

I've never looked at Bernie Taupin as a rock star. To me he's a poet with a banker's sensibilities and exquisite taste.

Taupin, who is best known as Elton John's songwriting partner, penned the words to so many famous songs that have immortalized him in the pantheon of lyricists. Bernie was different than most rock stars in that he didn't behave like one. He didn't trash hotel rooms, sleep with hordes of groupies or engage in bad-boy debauchery. He preferred drinking fine wines, collected fine art, raised horses, and invested his money in real estate and restaurants known for good food, ambience and location. He's more like an English version of Ralph Lauren.

Bernie is charming. He's a good listener, funny and is a wonderful host. Yet he's a very private man and holds his cards close to his vest. Bernie is like his lyrics – mysterious and deep. I didn't know him well enough to see the connection between his life and his lyrics. It doesn't matter because they mean something to everyone who hears them.

I took my pictures of Bernie in my living room in the late '70s. The light was soft and beautiful while he was sitting on the large burgundy sofa. We were on our way out for lunch but I grabbed my camera to capture the moment before we left. He was okay with that so I snapped away while he just connected with me through the lens. No posing, just staring at me with those deep dark orbs.

When I got the film back I was struck by Bernie's intensity and vulnerability. No pretense, no worries about the way he looked. It was Bernie just being himself and letting me record him as he was at that moment. A confidence that radiated from deep within where Rocket Man resided.

Left: A quiet moment with Bernie and the light was just right.

Above: Ringo and Bernie on a barge in Amsterdam. Silly boy.

Above right: Ringo with Bernie at his office in Los Angeles.

POLICE DEPT.
91825
OGNIR RRATS
CAR THIEF

Ringo TV Special

"Ringo" was an NBC television special, based loosely on Mark Twain's *The Prince and the Pauper*, but its real intent was to promote his latest album, *Bad Boy*.

Shot in and around Los Angeles over a twelve-day period in February 1978, the comedy/musical featured an all-star cast that included Art Carney, Vincent Price, John Ritter, Carrie Fisher, Angie Dickinson and a cameo appearance by George Harrison.

For the special, Ringo played the dual roles of himself, the rich and famous rock star, and his alter ego, the shy and nerdy Ognir Rrats (Ringo Starr spelled backwards). The finale featured Ringo and his Roadside Attraction band, performing live versions of three songs from *Bad Boy*: "Heart on My Sleeve," "Who Needs A Heart," and "A Man Like Me."

Ringo was very serious and focused on this shoot because it was the first television acting role that revolved around his music. Art Carney, who played Ringo's grumpy father, was so involved in his role that he didn't break character when the camera stopped rolling. He constantly ragged on his son, Ringo, in between takes. One time Ringo lifted his eyebrow and said, "That was mean." Art replied, "I'm supposed to be mean – I'm your father!" It was hilarious to watch the exchange.

Conversely, John Ritter was a classic cut-up who was thrilled to work with Ringo. Ritter was a staunch Beatles fan whose character Jack Tripper on "Three's Company" took the last name from the song "Day Tripper". Vincent Price was one of my childhood heroes from all those Roger Corman horror films. On screen he was such a strong presence but when the cameras stopped rolling, he turned into a sweet, elderly man. When I was introduced to him, Vincent said, "Ah, Nancy, I'm your namesake," referring to his "Ringo" role as Dr. Nancy.

Being given the job to shoot the publicity photos for the special meant a lot. It was a respect and responsibility as a photographer that I had never known before. I hired an assistant who helped me with lighting for the *TV Guide* and advertisement shoot. During the filming I just shot with my Nikon. It was more than a feather in my cap because not only did Ringo think I could handle the job, but his producers did as well.

Right: Ringo and Art Carney cutting up on the set.

Above: Taken on the publicity shoot for "Ringo".

Below: George and Ringo with Jeff Margolis, the director of "Ringo".

Left: Ringo walking on the set before shooting began.

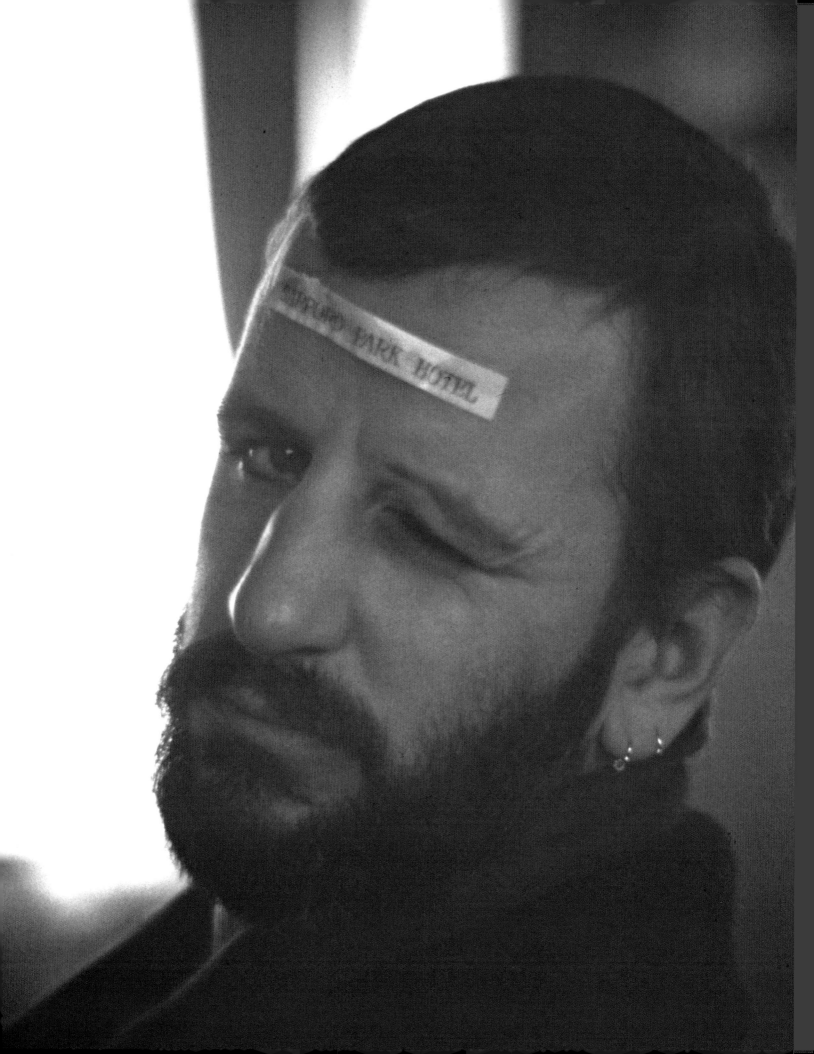

Japan

Japan was the perfect mixture of business and pleasure. While it was a business trip for Ringo, it was a mystical journey for me.

In October 1976, Ringo was hired as a spokesperson for a Japanese clothing company called Simple Life. He taped several television spots and recorded two jingles (written by Harry Nilsson) for Simple Life. We were on a huge press junket tour of Europe for *Rotogravure* and continued on to Japan.

We arrived in the middle of the night after a direct flight from Rome. A black limo whisked us to the Tokyo Hilton where they showed us to a large suite overlooking the city lights. In the morning Japan began to unfold before us and soon showed itself as breathtaking, bustling and friendly.

Ringo had visited the country a decade earlier when the Beatles toured there in the summer of 1966, but because security was so great, they were unable to leave their hotel. Local tradesmen were brought to them so they could at least buy some souvenirs. That was the extent of their exposure to the culture. This visit was completely different. There was a sense of discovery and wonderment for both of us.

We were given an interpreter and the country was ours for the taking – Tokyo, Kyoto, Sapporo and small cities in between. Every accommodation was first-class, every tour highly personalized and beyond what the public was allowed to see. For example, we were given a private tour of the Palace of the Emperor's Shogun Castle. Outside we encountered a touch of Beatlemania as a throng of teenage school girls in navy blue uniforms stood at a distance with cameras, giggling and snapping pictures of Ringo.

Ringo and I shot loads of film. The landscapes, architecture and buildings were magnificent but it was the people I found most interesting. While it may appear to most that the Japanese are reserved and quiet, I discovered most of their communication is done through their expressive eyes.

Pattie Boyd had told me before I left about a woman who sold antique kimonos but didn't remember exactly where. My guide had an idea and took me to an underground market where there were hundreds of vendors. Just as I had given up finding this lady, I turned and saw an old woman eating rice in the corner of her stall. I walked over to her and she was the one! She had her granddaughters bring out pile after pile of heavily-embroidered wedding kimonos, ceremonial and everyday silk kimonos. I bought over forty kimonos. Needless to say everyone received a kimono for Christmas that year.

At the Moss Temple in Kyoto, the gardeners were older men who dressed very neatly in white shirts, hats, vests, trousers and garden boots. I studied one gentlemen for the longest time. Once we made eye contact, I smiled and he nodded his head acknowledging me. I raised my camera and took his photo. He didn't smile for the camera, he continued his meticulous job of pruning.

Ringo enjoyed learning about the culture as well. We were served high tea by the Grand Tea Master of Japan. The ceremony was a cultural learning experience for us. Every movement of serving had a deep meaning of giving and friendship. Not your everyday 'cuppa tea'.

I haven't been back to Japan in three decades and I'm not sure I ever will. Everything about that first trip was magical and I don't want to ruin the perfect memory I have preserved all of these years.

Above: Choosing fabric
for my kimono.

Right: Hilary Gerrard
bundled up for the freezing
weather in Sapporo.

Above: An old man who found Ringo very interesting.

Above: Little school girls who were so excited to see a Beatle.

Above: Moss Temple Garden outside Kyoto.

Above: Japanese gardener.

Left & above: A private dinner in Tokyo. We were playing a Japanese dinner game that had something to do with a napkin on your head...didn't understand it then and don't now.

Ringo means 'apple' in Japanese.

Morocco

Life with Ringo had a nomad quality. We lived an average of six months a year in Los Angeles and the other half between Monte Carlo and other countries. During this time we were seeking to experience a different culture. We found what we were looking for in Morocco.

Even though Morocco is a quick trip across the Mediterranean Sea from the South of France, it might as well have been a million miles from our reality. Our lives revolved around work and then periods of down time. We had an exciting jet-set lifestyle that was incomparable. What we saw in Morocco was a complete contrast with our lives and gave us a little more perspective.

We left Nice in late May 1977 for Casablanca so that we could attend the Moroccan Folk Music Festival, a big annual event in Marrakesh. Our tour guide, Mustafa, was a former Olympic wrestling champion and a folk hero to the locals. "Welcome to Morocco, here's your car," he said in a thick accent as he opened the door to his old white Toyota, which had no air conditioning. Mustafa was a marvelous translator and proudly revealed the Moroccan people to us.

What appeared to be poverty to us was a way of life much like the early American Indians. We were in the desert so there was a limited amount of irrigated land. People lived in mud houses, like adobes, and there were men, women and children goat herding on the roads. There were no modern conveniences in sight.

The most amazing thing was the indomitable spirit of the people; despite their outward circumstances they seemed happy inside. There was a tremendous pride in their existence and that comes through in my photos.

One of my favorite pictures is a boy eating something standing next to an old man, wearing a suit jacket and a turban. The old man looked so elegant but when you examine him closely, his jacket is frayed and he has a safety pin holding it closed. Another intriguing shot was of a young man with a tilted hat, twisting red yarn and looking like a character out of a storybook.

Walking through Fez to the heart of the city was incredible because parts haven't changed for centuries. The children of the streets were beautiful. They freely wandered around begging or toting bales of yarn on their heads. I stopped at one doorway and three little boys popped up smiling. Each face was covered with a different color because they were working, churning the huge pots of dye. Morocco didn't know anything about child labor laws in 1977.

On one of our last days in Morocco we ventured to the tip of the Sahara Desert near Rissani, an army town. We heard explosions in the distance and Ringo queried Mustafa about the noise. He explained that two tribes were at war. "They're fighting over water, they're fighting over sand, they're fighting over a goat," Mustafa said. "They will probably never stop fighting."

Despite this experience, we left Morocco filled with a profound peacefulness.

Above: Overlooking the
Tinihir Valley at sunset.

Top left: Children who worked in the Dyers Mart, Fez.

Top right: Worker in the Dyers Mart, Fez.

Right: The very young and the very old, Marrakesh.

The Last Waltz

The Last Waltz was a rock 'n' roll version of a high school reunion. It was a gathering of old friends to toast and send off The Band, who were calling it quits after years of intense touring.

There was a lot of electricity surrounding the Thanksgiving Day 1976 concert, which took place in San Francisco. The four-hour concert was captured on celluloid by famed New York film director Martin Scorsese, who talked fast and walked even faster. He seemed to be everywhere at the same time.

In addition to Ringo, the luminaries included Bob Dylan, Van Morrison, Neil Young, Emmylou Harris, Joni Mitchell, Muddy Waters, Eric Clapton, Neil Diamond, Dr. John, Ron Wood, Stephen Stills, Charlie Daniels and Paul Butterfield. It was one of the most spectacular concerts in rock history. Everyone who was anyone in music was there to witness the event. A chartered commercial jet took Ringo and me along with the who's who of Los Angeles up to San Francisco.

Promoter Bill Graham, who had a long and enduring association with The Band, hosted the event at his Winterland Ballroom. Bill did everything in grand style. An audience of 5,000 people was served turkey dinners and that was followed by ballroom dancing with music provided by the Berkeley Promenade Orchestra. Poets Lawrence Ferlinghetti and Michael McClure rounded off the cultural affair with poetry readings.

I brought my sleek SX-70 Polaroid camera because I knew it was going to be a fast moving night and it would take too much time to load film in a bulky camera. With the SX-70 built-in flash I could snap a photo, the camera would spit it out and I could give it away or quickly stash it in my pocket. I was lucky to catch Bob Dylan laughing at a funny comment made by someone in the room. The photo is memorable because I had never before seen Bob so much as crack a smile.

When Scorsese had cameras ready to roll, The Band opened with "Up on Cripple Creek," followed by a rundown of their most popular songs, including "The Shape I'm In", "The Weight", and "The Night They Drove Old Dixie Down." They were then joined by a succession of guest artists, including Ringo, who drummed on an inspired version of "I Shall Be Released." Around 2:15 a.m., only The Band performed a final encore, "Don't Do It." It was the last time the original group was on stage together.

Throughout the night Ringo and I wandered to and from the backstage area visiting with musicians, friends and significant others. There was a camaraderie among the musicians; they all had an artistic connection that was strong. When they were on stage, they were sharing with each other and thus their audience. I know that sounds deep, but only music can transport us to a place that is all our own and at the same time share the experience with a mass of people.

When the concert ended the private party rocked on for several more hours. I remember falling asleep sitting in a chair, Ringo shaking me, then rushing to catch the plane back to Los Angeles. What a night!

Top Left: Mac and Ringo being silly in the shower backstage.

Above: Mac and Lorraine Rebennack.

Left: Bobby Neuwirth, a talented singer, songwriter, record producer.

Top: Rick Danko.

Above right: Richard Emanuel and his lady.

Above: Charlie Daniels and Ronee Blakley.

Right: Eric Clapton.

Above left: Pattie Boyd and me.

Above: Ronee Blakley and Lorraine Rebennack.

Left: Me, two unknown ladies, Pattie Boyd and Rita Wolf.

Above right: Betsy Asher and
Joni Mitchell with a friend.

Right: Rita Wolf and Pattie Boyd.

The Band

The Band is one of my all-time favorite groups. The Canadian-American rockers backed Bob Dylan for his 1965-66 world tour and were more popular with rock critics and music journalists than with the general public. There was such beauty in the simplicity of their musicianship and I loved the storytelling in their songs. The Band seemed to belong to another place and time. Their work was a reminder that our musical roots evolved from Scotland, Ireland and England, and morphed into American hill country fables during the Civil War. They were a breath of fresh air in the psychedelic era.

We met up again in 1989 at a charity concert called "This Country's Rockin'." The show was filmed in the cavernous Silverdome in Pontiac, Michigan, where I was hired by the promoter to shoot publicity photos. I created a Rogues Gallery, a makeshift studio in the backstage area, to take portraits of all the acts before and after their performances.

Because I had known The Band from *The Last Waltz* performance, particularly drummer Levon Helm, they were glad to see me again and were wonderful hosts. The boys in The Band were a down-home bunch, talking about where to get the best fried chicken in town, how much they paid for a heifer, or the latest music project that Levon was developing for cable television. Sophisticated country/city boys.

The fun thing about shooting a Rogues Gallery is that whoever is in front of the camera has a peanut gallery behind the photographer giving them loads of grief – anything to crack the veneer of the subject. Also, the pictures I shot of them in rehearsal are amongst my favorites because they were not on the spot. They were just doing what they do – making beautiful music and putting smiles on thousands of faces.

Above: Garth, Levon and Danko in the Rogue's Gallery.

Right: Garth Hudson setting up his instruments at soundcheck. Charlie Daniels in the background.

Far right: Rick Danko at soundcheck.

Rick Danko
1942~1999

Above: The great
pyramid at Chitzen Itza.

The Yucatan

Today the Yucatan is one of the most popular tourist destinations in the world, but in the 1970s it was still a remote and unseen land that preserved a lot of its authentic Mayan culture.

In April 1977, Ringo, me, his manager Hilary Gerrard and my girlfriend, Susin S. Fair decided to take a trip together. We wanted to go someplace that had a tropical setting and a beach but was isolated from most of civilization. We flew to Mexico City then hopped a small-engined aircraft to Cozumel, where our plane landed on a dirt runway close to town. We were greeted by a man whose office was a cinder block hut that represented the airlines and sold Orangina soda out of an icebox. We were taken by taxi to the only large hotel on the other side of the island.

Hilary was a renaissance man and financial genius from England. Every time I asked him what he was up to, he had either come back from some exotic locale like Katmandu or had visited with the Dalai Lama. His slight build, bald head and professorial looks made him stand out in a crowd. Hilary chain-smoked and usually had a cigarette in one hand and Tibetan prayer beads in the other, which was the perfect example of his dual personality. Susin was one of my oldest friends. We had met when we were eighteen and modeling in Manhattan. At this particular time she was writing for *The Village Voice*.

Turned out we had a ball. We spent our days reading and relaxing on the beach, toured the Mayan ruins and took a day trip to Chitzen Itza to climb the steps of the ancient temple. One day we drove in our rented yellow Volkswagen Thing to a remote part of the island to watch a solar eclipse. With the top down and a hand drawn map to our destination, we were off on our next adventure. By the time we were deep into the jungle on a deserted dirt road, the wind started to howl and rain pelted down. Ringo was driving when we hit a deep hole and the axle snapped. We were rescued a few hours later by some friendly French Canadian tourists, who drove us back to the hotel.

After seven days in the Yucatan Ringo became restless. He woke up one morning and said, "Get me off this island. I don't care how you do it, but get me outta here."

In a matter of hours I managed to book a single-engined plane to Merida that seated six people. Our party of four, the two pilots and our embarrassing amount of luggage put us well over the plane's weight capacity. Despite that and a looming tropical storm, no one could talk Ringo into staying another day. The pounding storm forced us to fly so low that the bottom of the plane was brushing against the tops of the trees. I was trying to calm Susin down, who was sure that we were going to go crash in the jungle and our remains would never be found. Hilary was holding Tibetan prayer beads up against his third eye, furiously chanting and wishing for a cigarette. While everyone was frantic and on the verge of breaking down, Ringo was as calm as could be. He said very matter-of-factly, "Don't worry, it's not my time to go, so we'll all be fine."

Above: Hilary smiling before take off from Cozumel.

Above right: Polaroids were our passion wherever we were.

Below right: My girlfriend, Susin, took this of us looking very much on holiday.

Sunset on the beach in Cozumel.

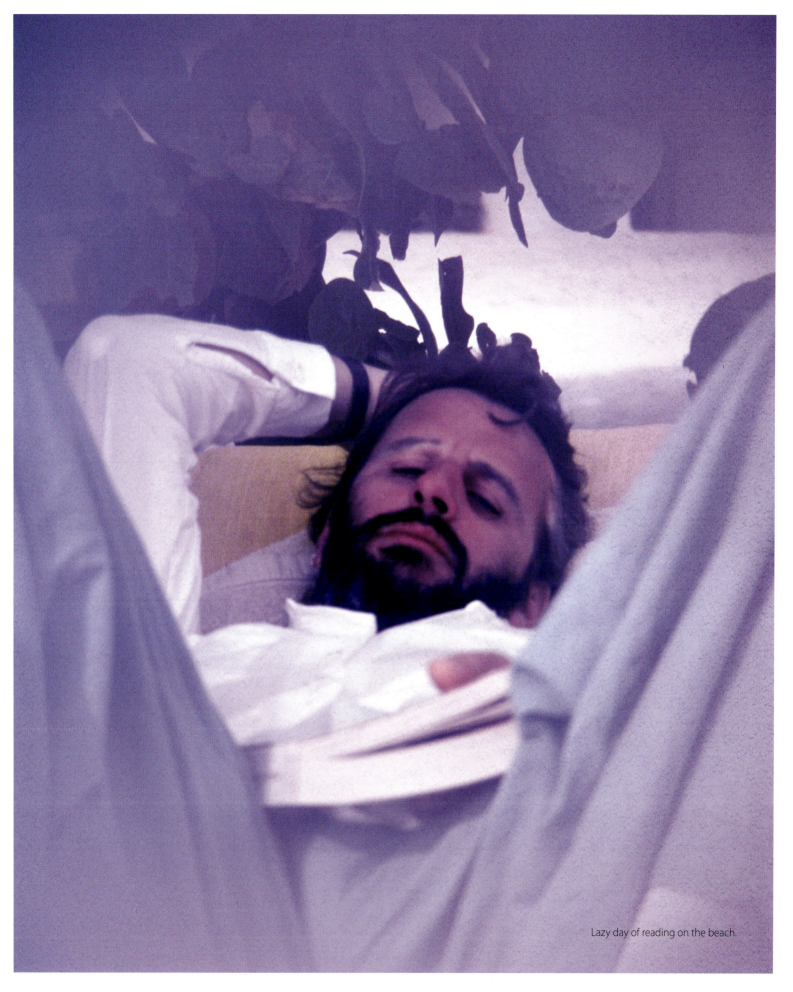

Lazy day of reading on the beach.

Left: Catching a sun beam.

Above: I love this shot because
I'm reflected in his sunglasses.

Caveman

There's an old saying that comedy is the mirror image of tragedy – such was the case with *Caveman*.

The movie certainly seemed to have all the right ingredients: a funny premise, a strong cast, an exotic locale and a former Beatle as the film's top-billed actor.

Principal photography was slated in mid-February 1980 in Durango, Mexico, but a clash with Customs officials when Ringo entered the country seemed ominous. Ringo was strip-searched by Customs as a result of Paul McCartney's infamous marijuana bust in Japan just a month before. I saw Mexico's finest when I joined Ringo two weeks later. Armed Federales surrounded the set for the duration of the location shoot. The assistant director told me they were for our protection from rebel soldiers who in the past had pillaged food, animals, equipment and had even kidnapped women.

The prehistoric slapstick comedy was set in "One Zillion Years B.C." and featured a mere fifteen words of dialogue. The picture was helmed by actor-turned-director Carl Gottlieb and co-starred Dennis Quaid, Shelley Long, John Matuszak, Avery Schreiber and Barbara Bach, whom I had known in my modeling days. The cast was fun and loose, which was a positive. The five-week shoot required long hours and was physically demanding because of the slapstick humor and terrain.

Ringo immediately bonded with Dennis Quaid, and the two acted like juvenile brothers. John Matuszak, who stood 6 feet 8 inches and weighed 308 pounds, was a gentle giant who was practiced in the art of flirtation.

Shelley Long was sweet and kind, and on the periphery of fame. Barbara Bach, an ex-James Bond girl, was the glamorous Neanderthal woman.

The film was mostly shot in the desert about a half-hour into the heart of the Durango badlands. I was very interested in the special effects because everything was so big and over the top. The animated dinosaur that Ringo rode in the movie is one of my favorite images captured on set.

When *Caveman* wrapped in late March 1980, so did our seven-year relationship. I didn't hear from Ringo for two weeks. He and co-star Barbara Bach had fallen in love on the set.

"I'm with Barbara now," Ringo told me when he got back to Los Angeles. I went to visit them at the Beverly Wilshire Hotel to bring a box of pictures I had taken while on the set of *Caveman*. It was strange visiting the man I had lived with just a month earlier and was betrothed to marry sitting with another woman, acting like a couple in love. As I waited for the elevator I looked down the long hallway thinking of all the times through the years we had stayed in this hotel, possibly in that very same suite.

The ding of the elevator doors opened and snapped me out of my reverie. With tears in my eyes I pressed lobby button and remembered Ringo saying to me, "You can't fight lightning."

No, you can't. My lightning, Eddie Barnes, finally struck me a decade later and it feels real good when you meet and marry the right one.

Left: Riding the wild dinosaur in the Mexican desert.

Left: John Matuszak was a doll and a flirt with the camera.

Below left: Carl Gottlieb, director and writer of *Caveman*. A brilliant sweetheart.

Above: Not only was John tall but he had a good butt!

Above: Shelley Long on a break from filming.

Left: Dennis and Ringo on the beach in Mexico.

Right: What a heartthrob!

Left: Dennis Quaid,
exhausted from a long
day of shooting in the
Mexican desert.

Above: Ringo's hat was
sporting a plastic leaf
that looked like cannabis.

Left: Matuszak and the beautiful Barbara Bach.

Above: Ringo was into all facets of filmmaking.

Afterword

I hope you have come away from *A Dose of Rock 'n' Roll* with a memory, a smile or even an insight into the 1970s. Maybe you were there. If so I hope you appreciate the care that was put into these chapters.

Here I am more than thirty years later still feeling like the girl on these pages...young, full of hope and still creating through photography. Growing older has brought many gifts...wisdom, knowledge, peace, aches and pains, glasses, two poodles and a Chrysler minivan.

My life is still an adventure. My photography ranges from music CD packages and fashion to whatever moves me. Family and friends take the front seat of my daily life. My husband, Eddie and I travel quite a lot, be it Europe, New York, New Jersey, Los Angeles or any beach that calls to us.

The 1970s was a time that will never be again, like the Roaring '20s. It was a breakthrough like manna from heaven. I guess that's why our present generation is replicating everything from the music to fashion to hairstyles. I share clothes and memories with my nieces, and my husband loves to turn on the nephews to the music that still sounds better than anything we hear today. Jeez, I sound like an old fogy.

I wish you happiness, peace and love.

Design: Ben Gibbs - Motion Design, United Kingdom
Printer: Star Standard Industries Pte Ltd., Singapore
Printing Equipment: Four colour litho on Roland Speedmaster
Inks: Toyochem
Page size: 11 inches x 9 inches
Text: Bookman Old Style 9.5pt
Text paper: 170 gsm Stora Enso Matt Art
End papers: 140 gsm Woodfree
Dust jacket: 135 gsm Glossy Art